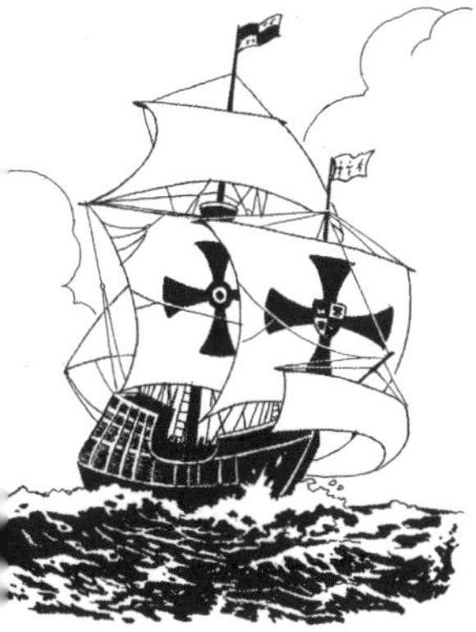

In 1493, on his second voyage to the New World, Christopher Columbus lands the first Criollo cattle on Hispaniola. Also known as Black Cattle, the Criollo were a hardy breed from ... t country of Southern Spain ... r, Gregorio de Villal... transported genera... tional offspring from Columbus's original herd to Mexico.

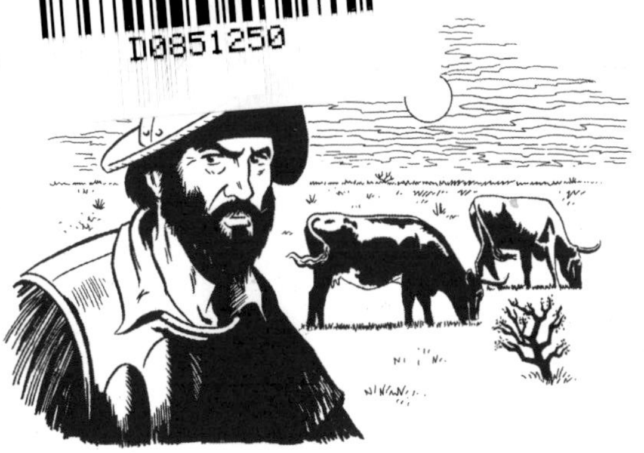

In 1540, 500 Criollo from Villalobos's herd accompany Francisco Vásquez de Coronado y Luján in his quest to find the Seven Cities of Cibola. Along the way Coronado leaves Criollo in New Mexico, Arizona, and Texas. The Criollo were self-dependent, prolific breeders who later, when crossbred with British bloodlines would produce the most recognized and historically significant cattle breed in American history . . .



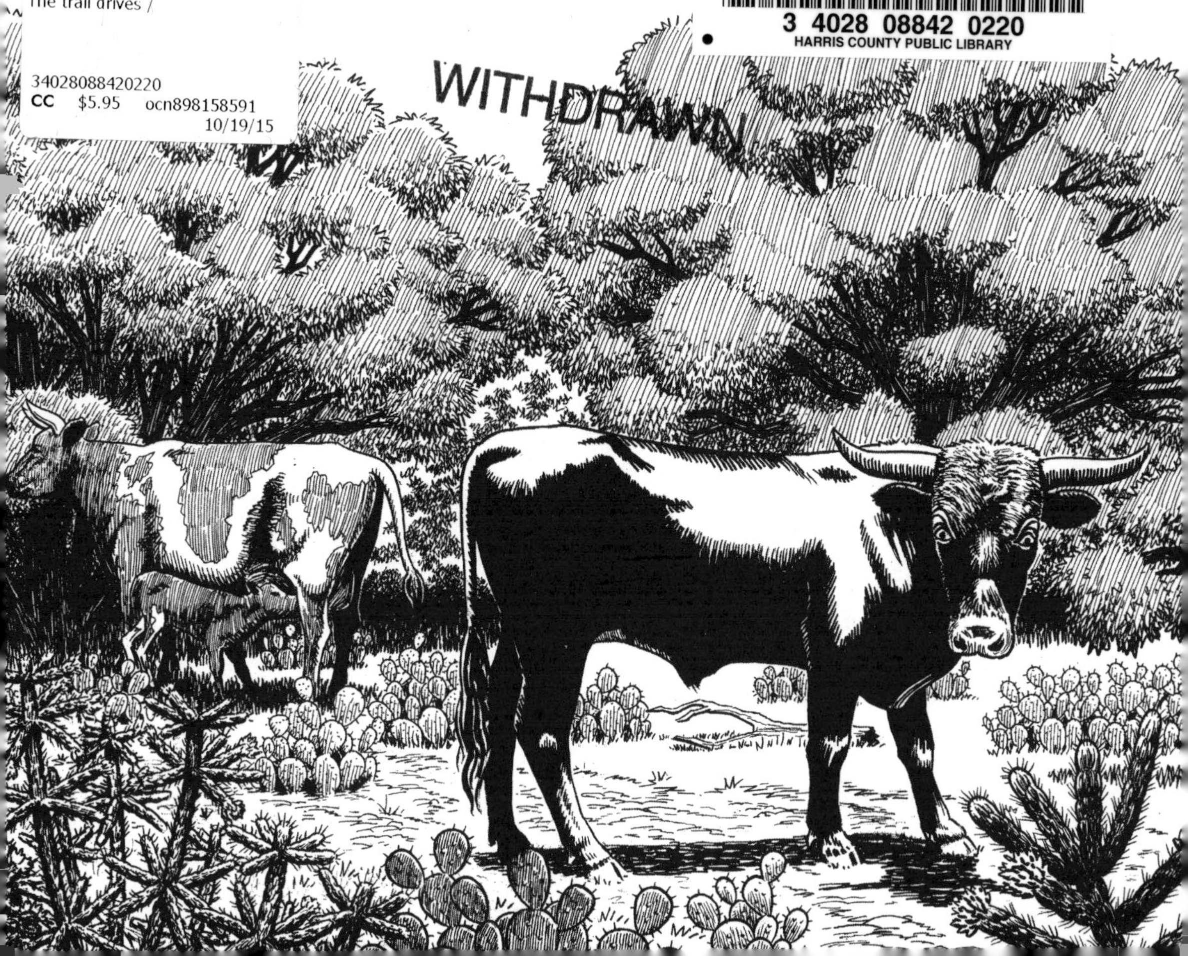

"THE **TEXAS LONGHORN** MADE MORE HISTORY THAN ANY OTHER BREED OF CATTLE THE CIVILIZED WORLD HAS KNOWN. HOWEVER SUPPLANTED OR HOWEVER DISPARAGED BY EVOLVING STANDARDS AND GENERATIONS, HE WILL REMAIN THE BEDROCK ON WHICH THE HISTORY OF THE COW COUNTRY OF AMERICA IS FOUNDED...
— J. FRANK DOBIE, **THE LONGHORNS**

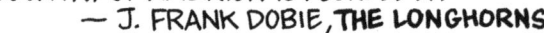

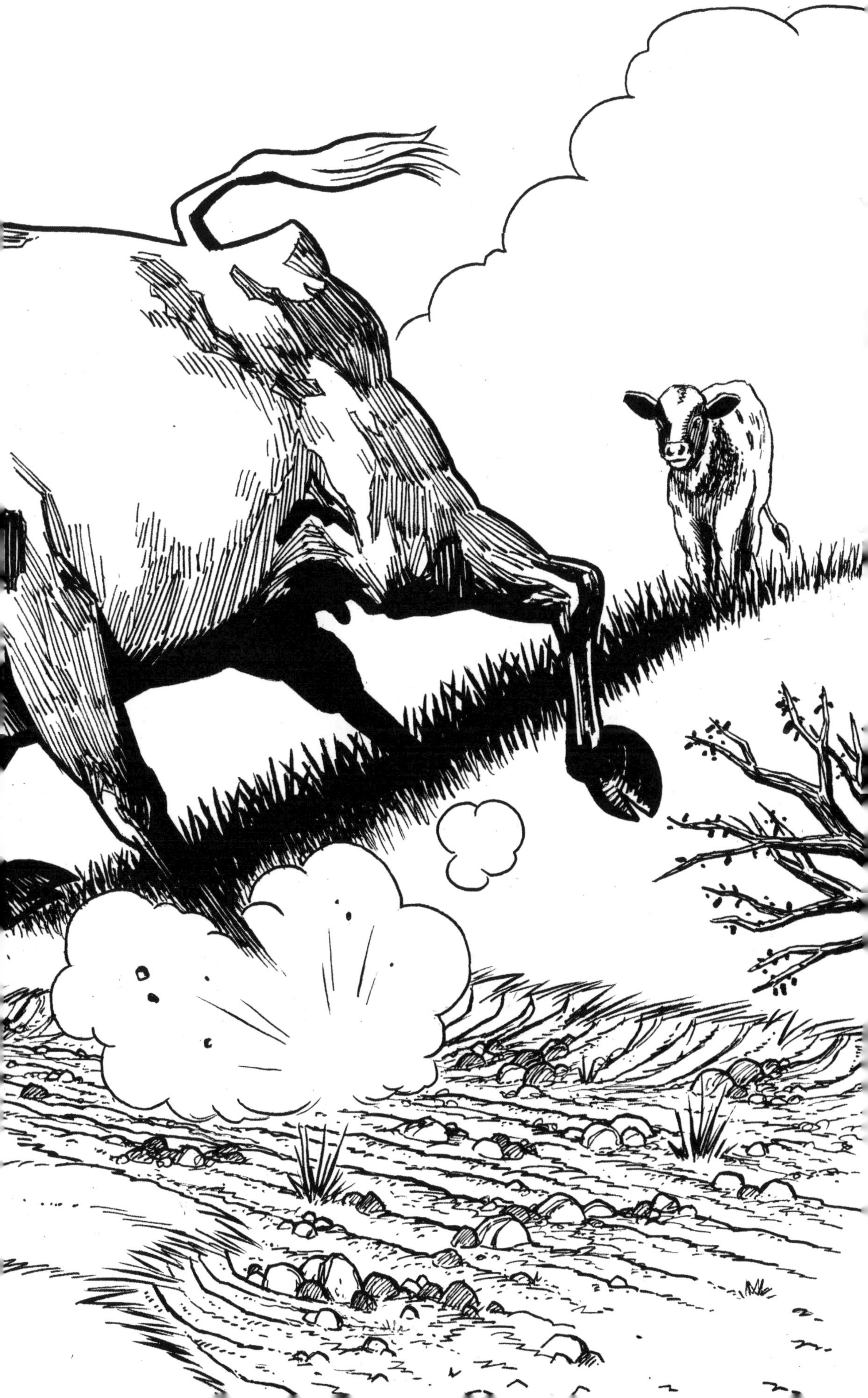

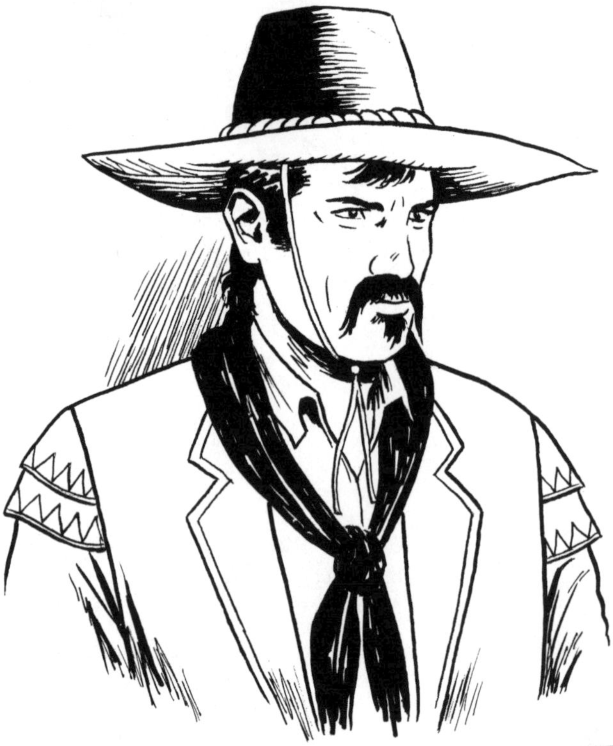

MEXICAN **VAQUEROS** WERE THE FIRST WORKING COW MEN IN NORTH AMERICA AND FORERUNNER TO THE COWBOY. BY THE TIME ANGLO SETTLERS ARRIVED IN TEXAS, VAQUEROS HAD BEEN "ROUNDING-UP" STRAY OR WILD CATTLE FROM THE BRUSH COUNTRY OR **BRASADA** FOR MORE THAN TWO CENTURIES.

A VAQUERO'S WORK APPAREL INCLUDED **LEATHER LEGGINS** THAT COVERED HIM FROM ANKLE TO WAIST, **GLOVES** THAT EXTENDED PAST HIS WRISTS, AND A **WIDE-BRIMMED HAT** THAT COULD BE CINCHED TIGHT UNDER HIS CHIN. THIS **ARMOR** SERVED TO PROTECT HIM FROM PRICKLY PEAR, CATCLAW, SPANISH DAGGER, OR THE VIOLENT CUT OF ROPE ACROSS HIS LEG BY A LASSOED COW OR HORSE...

THE VAQUERO'S **ROPE** WAS SHORT AS HE COULD NEVER COUNT ON A WIDE ENOUGH ALLEY IN WHICH TO SWING IT WHEN HUNTING IN THE BRASADA. **TOE FENDERS** KEPT HIS STIRRUPS FROM HANGING IN THE BRUSH AND THE HIGH **POMMEL** OF HIS SADDLE ACTED AS A CLEAT TO SECURE ANY ROPED BEAST...

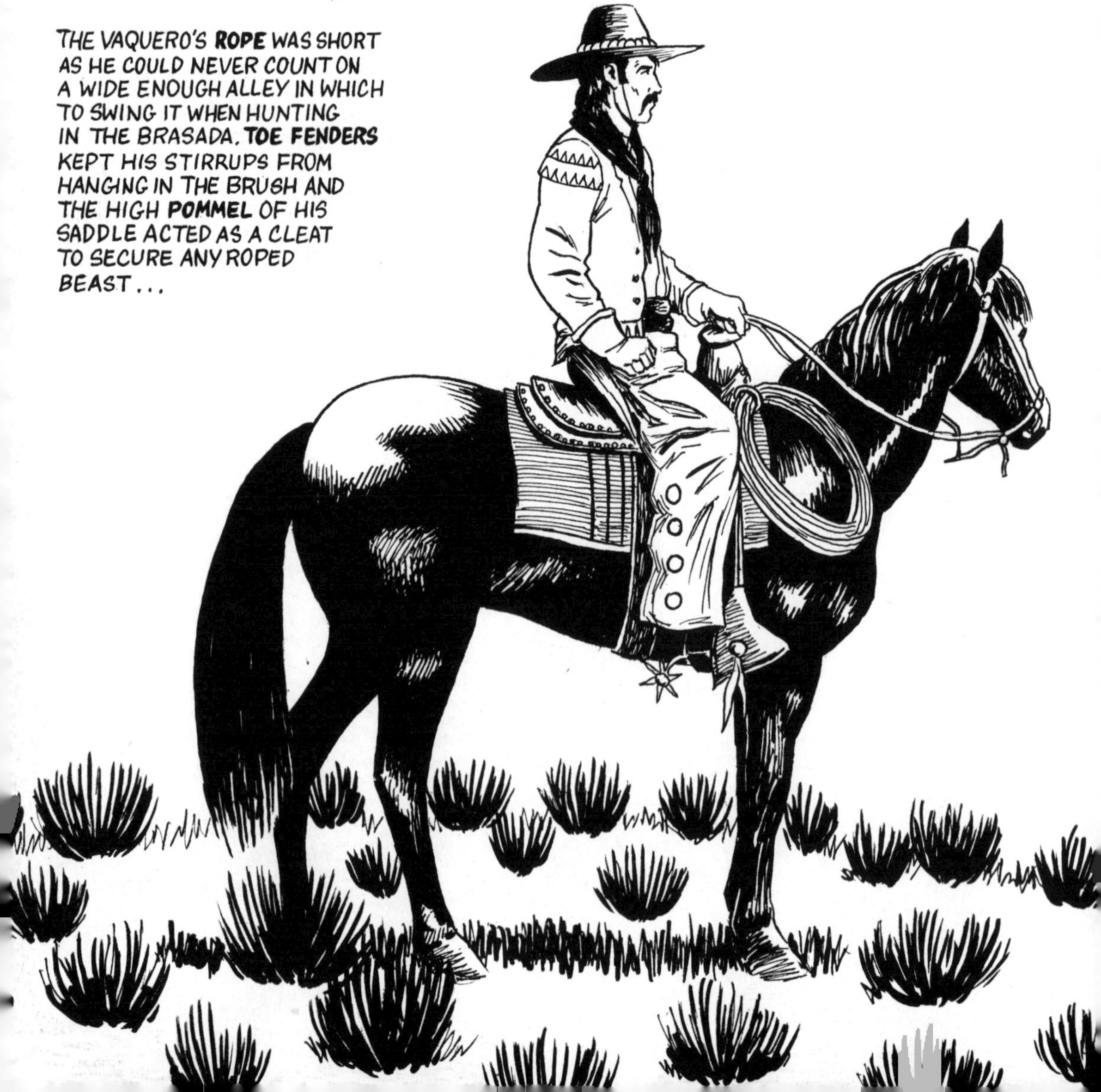

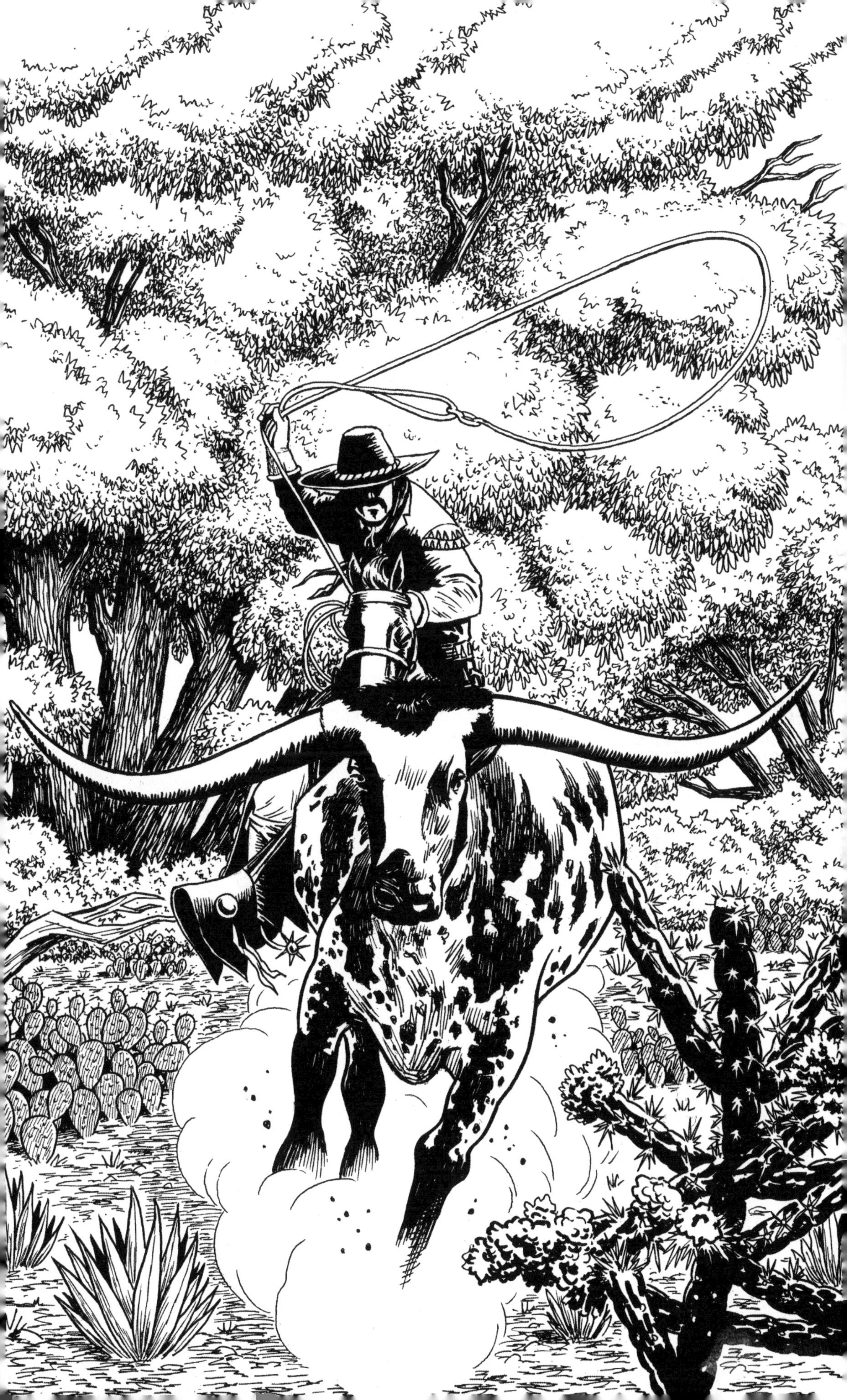

IN 1846, **EDWARD PIPER** TRAILED 1,000 HEAD OF CATTLE ON AN EMIGRANT ROUTE KNOWN AS THE **SHAWNEE TRAIL**. **PIPER'S** DRIVE IS THE FIRST RECORDED NORTH-SOUTH CATTLE DRIVE OUT OF **TEXAS**. THE MAIN **TEXAS** STEM PASSED THROUGH **AUSTIN, WACO** AND **DALLAS**. THE **SHAWNEE TRAIL** WAS ALSO KNOWN AS **PRESTON ROAD** (**TEXAS**), THE **TEXAS TRAIL** (**OKLAHOMA**), AND THE **KANSAS TRAIL** (**KANSAS, MISSOURI**).

IN 1855, FARMERS IN **MISSOURI** SET UP VIGILANCE COMMITTEES TO PROTECT THEIR LAND AND LIVESTOCK FROM A **TICK-BORNE DISEASE** CARRIED BY **TEXAS CATTLE**. QUARANTINES ENACTED BY **KANSAS** AND **MISSOURI** LEGISLATURES SOON FORCED THE GREAT HERDS FARTHER WEST, AWAY FROM THE HEAVILY POPULATED EASTERN CENTERS . . .

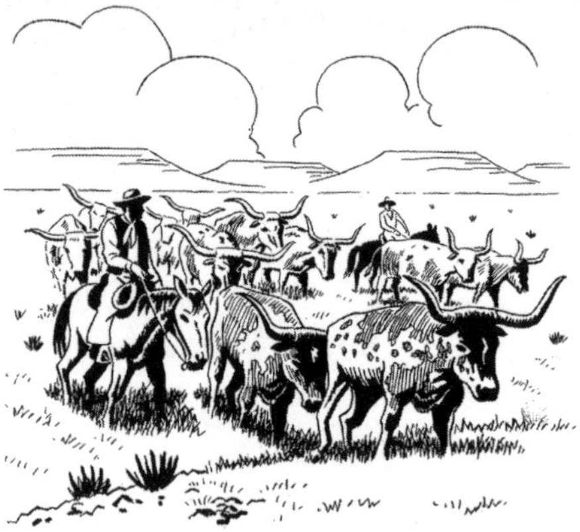

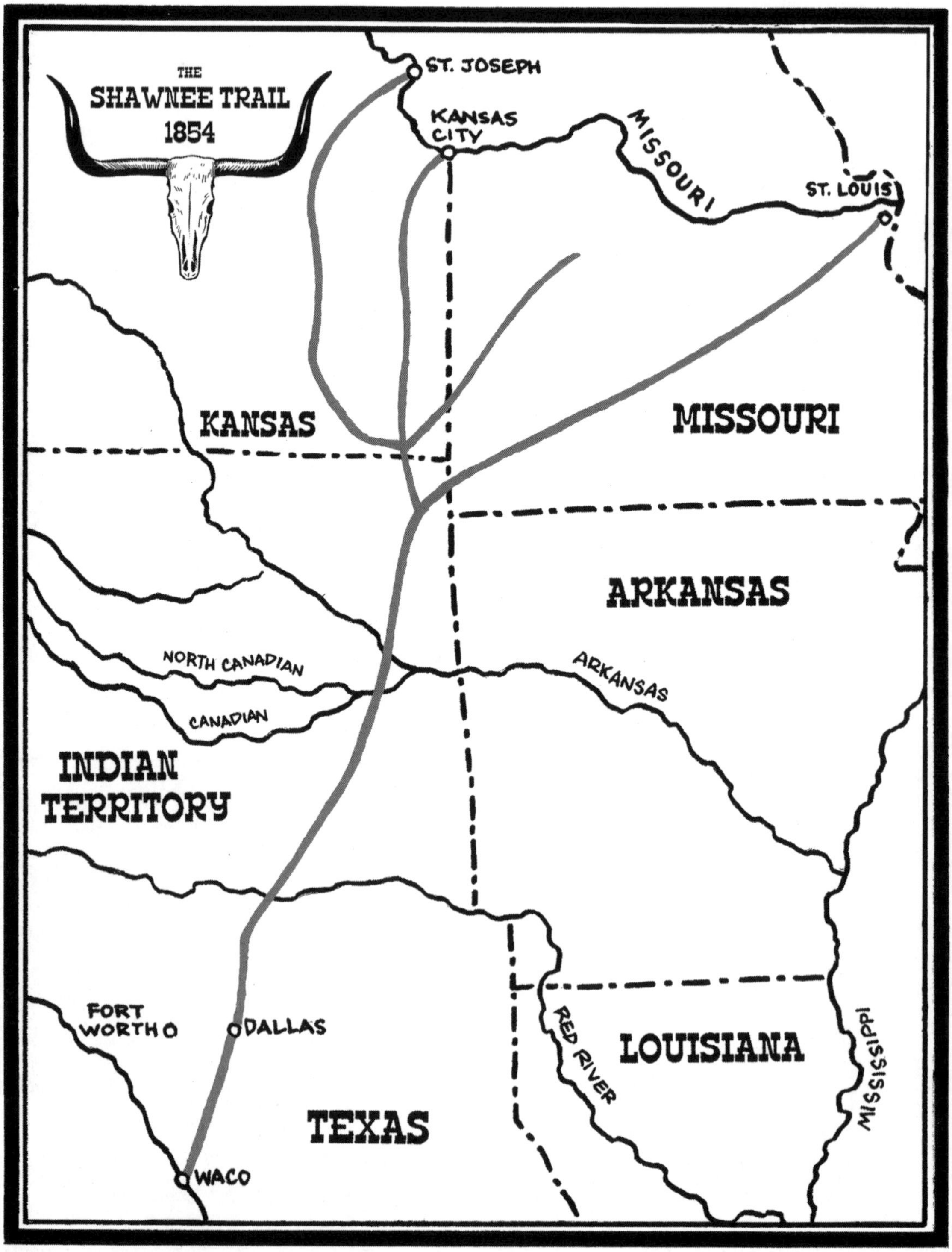
THE
SHAWNEE TRAIL
1854
ST. JOSEPH
KANSAS CITY
MISSOURI
ST. LOUIS
KANSAS
MISSOURI
ARKANSAS
NORTH CANADIAN
ARKANSAS
CANADIAN
INDIAN TERRITORY
FORT WORTH
DALLAS
RED RIVER
LOUISIANA
MISSISSIPPI
TEXAS
WACO

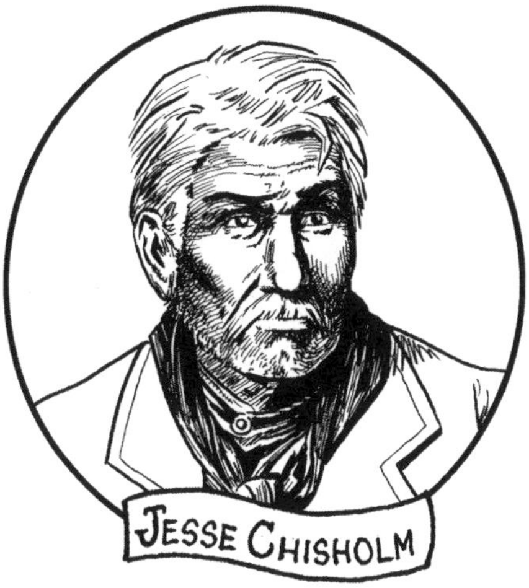
JESSE CHISHOLM

BY 1867, DROVERS FOUND THEIR HERDS INCREASINGLY DELAYED OR TURNED BACK ALONG THE **SHAWNEE TRAIL** DUE TO FEAR OF **TEXAS FEVER**. FOR MANY, THE QUARANTINES AND FINES SEEMED TO MARK THE END OF TRAILING CATTLE NORTH OUT OF TEXAS. THAT SAME YEAR, **O. W. WHEELER** TRAILED 2,400 TEXAS LONGHORNS FROM SAN ANTONIO TO FORT ARBUCKLE. WHEELER WANTED TO WINTER HIS BEEVES ON THE GRASS-RICH PLAINS BEFORE TRAILING THEM TO CALIFORNIA. AT A TRADING POST ON THE **NORTH CANADIAN RIVER** OPERATED BY **JESSE CHISHOLM**, WHEELER DISCOVERED THAT THE TRADER'S HEAVILY TRAVELED FREIGHT TRAIL OFFERED A CLEAR ROUTE TO PRESENT-DAY **WICHITA, KANSAS**. WHEELER TRAILED HIS HERD SAFELY ACROSS CHISHOLM'S ROUTE, THEN FOLLOWED A RECENTLY SURVEYED TRAIL TO **ABILENE, KANSAS**. IN THE YEARS THAT FOLLOWED, TEXAS COWBOYS BEGAN REFERRING TO THEIR ROUTE FROM TEXAS TO ABILENE AS: THE **CHISHOLM TRAIL** . . .

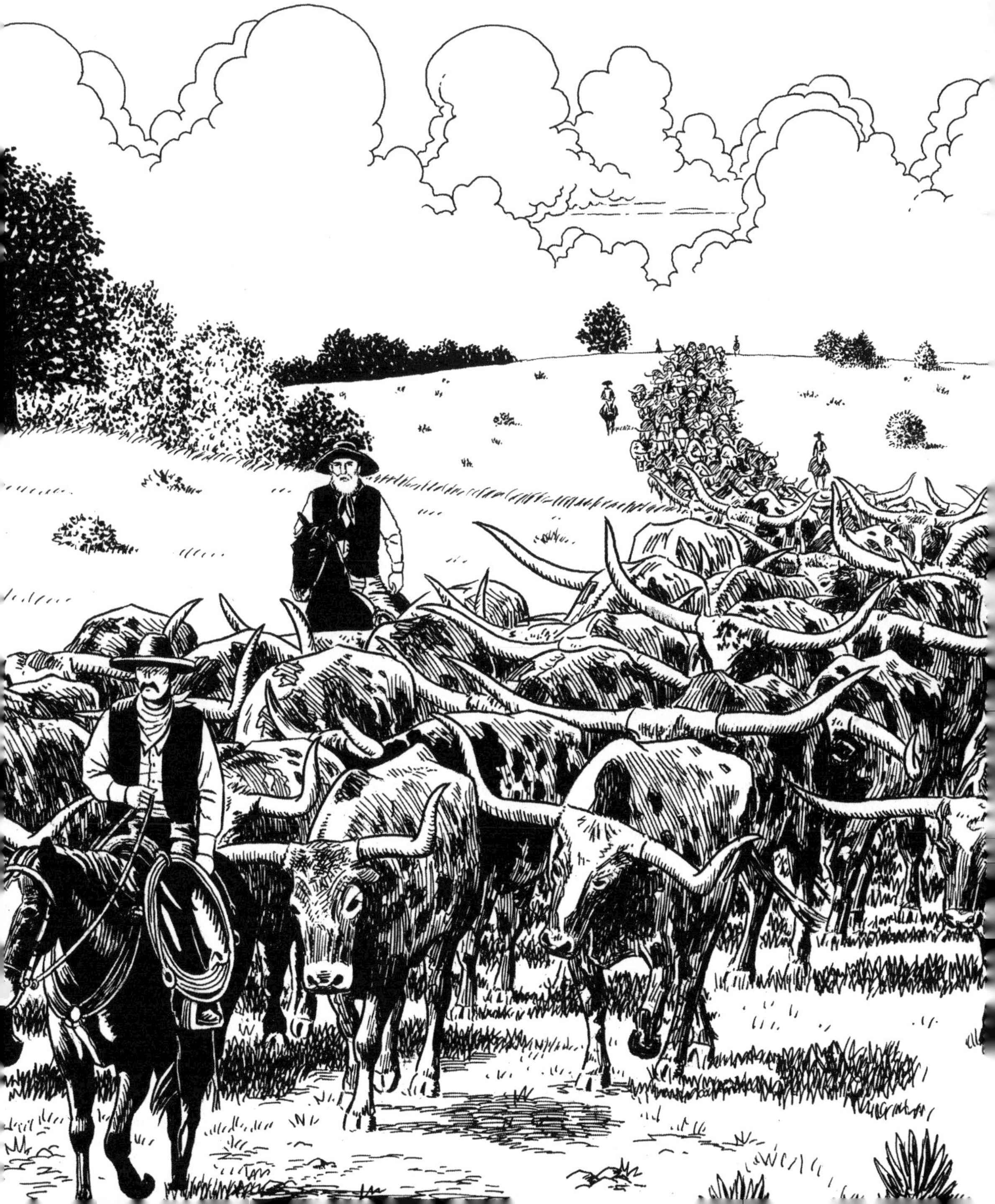

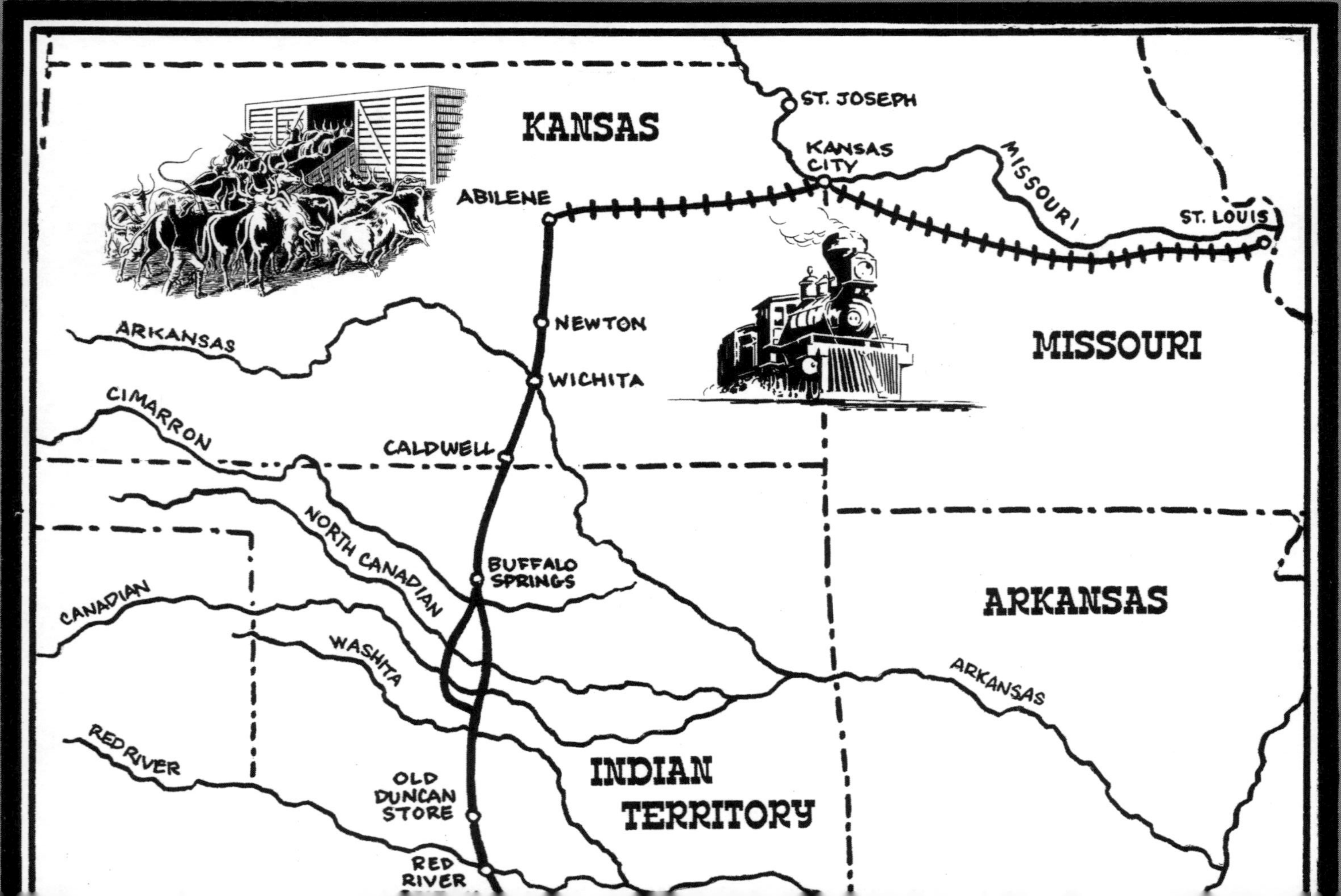
KANSAS
ST. JOSEPH
KANSAS CITY
MISSOURI
ST. LOUIS
ABILENE
NEWTON
WICHITA
ARKANSAS
CIMARRON
CALDWELL
MISSOURI
NORTH CANADIAN
BUFFALO SPRINGS
CANADIAN
WASHITA
ARKANSAS
ARKANSAS
RED RIVER
OLD DUNCAN STORE
RED RIVER
INDIAN TERRITORY

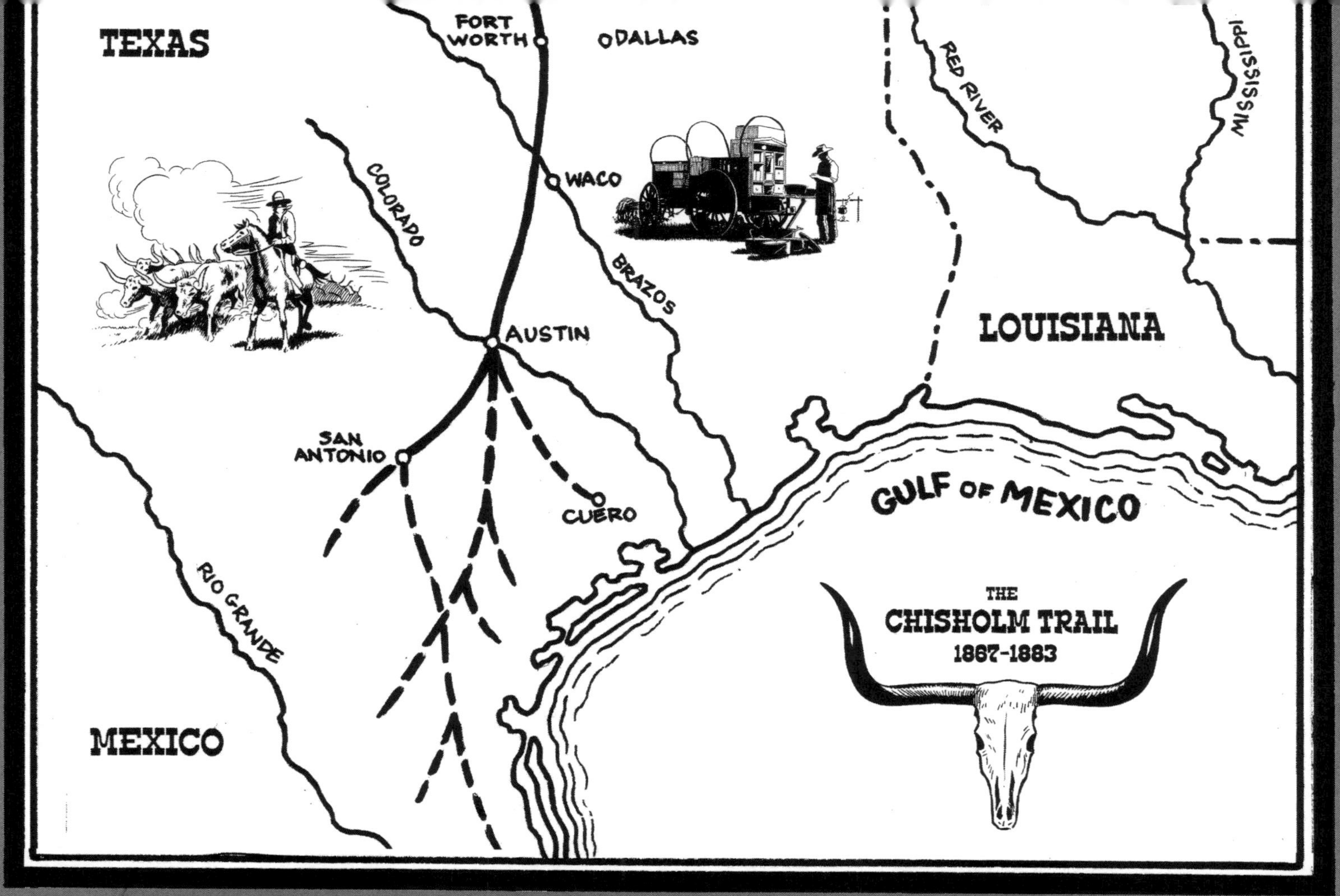
TEXAS
FORT WORTH
DALLAS
RED RIVER
MISSISSIPPI
WACO
COLORADO
BRAZOS
AUSTIN
LOUISIANA
SAN ANTONIO
CUERO
GULF OF MEXICO
RIO GRANDE
THE
CHISHOLM TRAIL
1867-1883
MEXICO

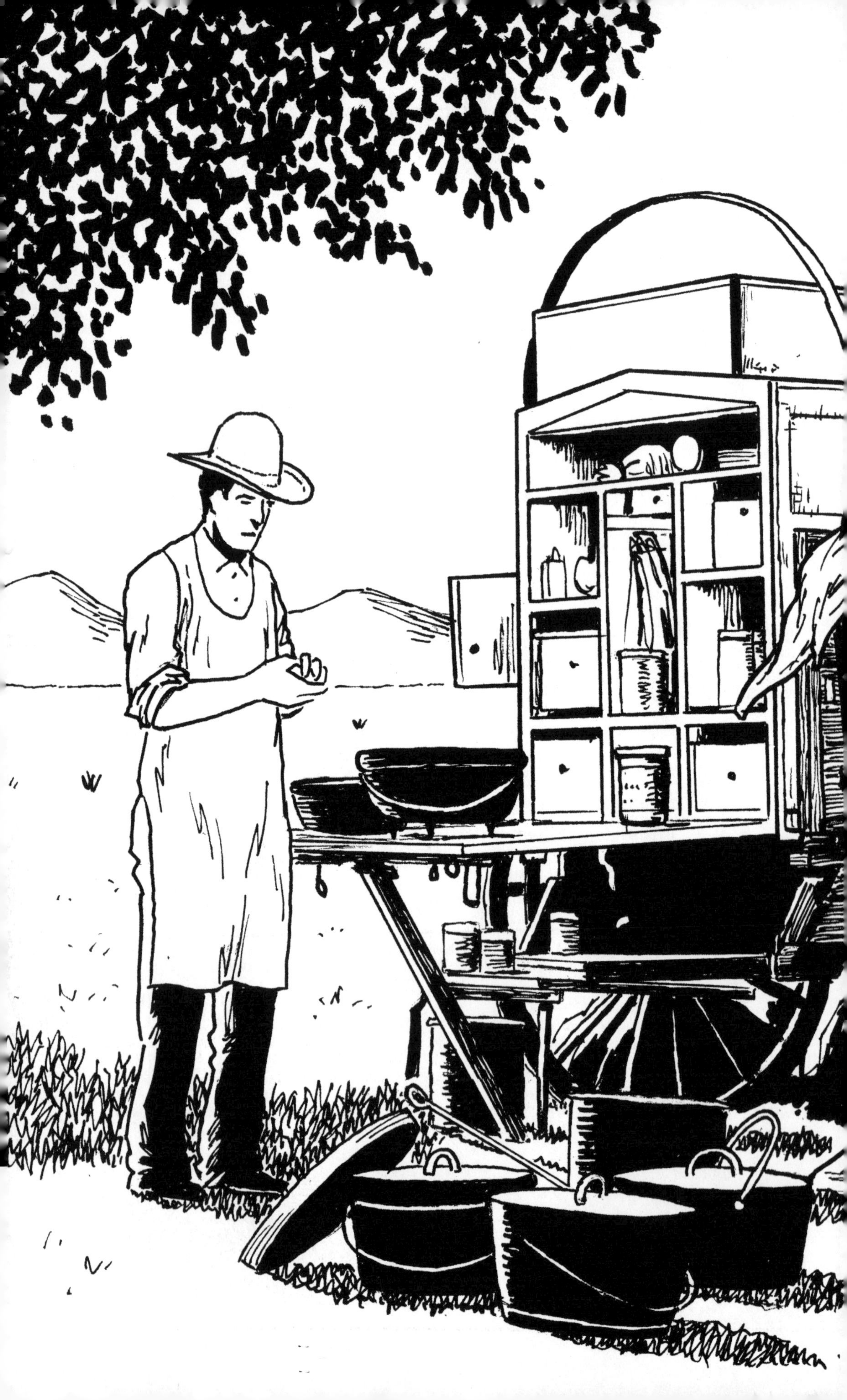

IN 1866, **CHARLES GOODNIGHT** MODIFIED A MULTI-PURPOSE **STUDEBAKER** WAGON INTO A **MOBILE KITCHEN**. AN ASTUTE BUSINESSMAN, GOODNIGHT REALIZED THAT GOOD FOOD AND AN ACCOMPLISHED COOK WOULD ENTICE THE BEST COWBOYS TO HIRE ON WITH HIM. THE MODIFIED WAGON BECAME KNOWN AS THE **CHUCK WAGON**; THE NAME DERIVED FROM A CUT OF BEEF CALLED THE **"CHUCK."**

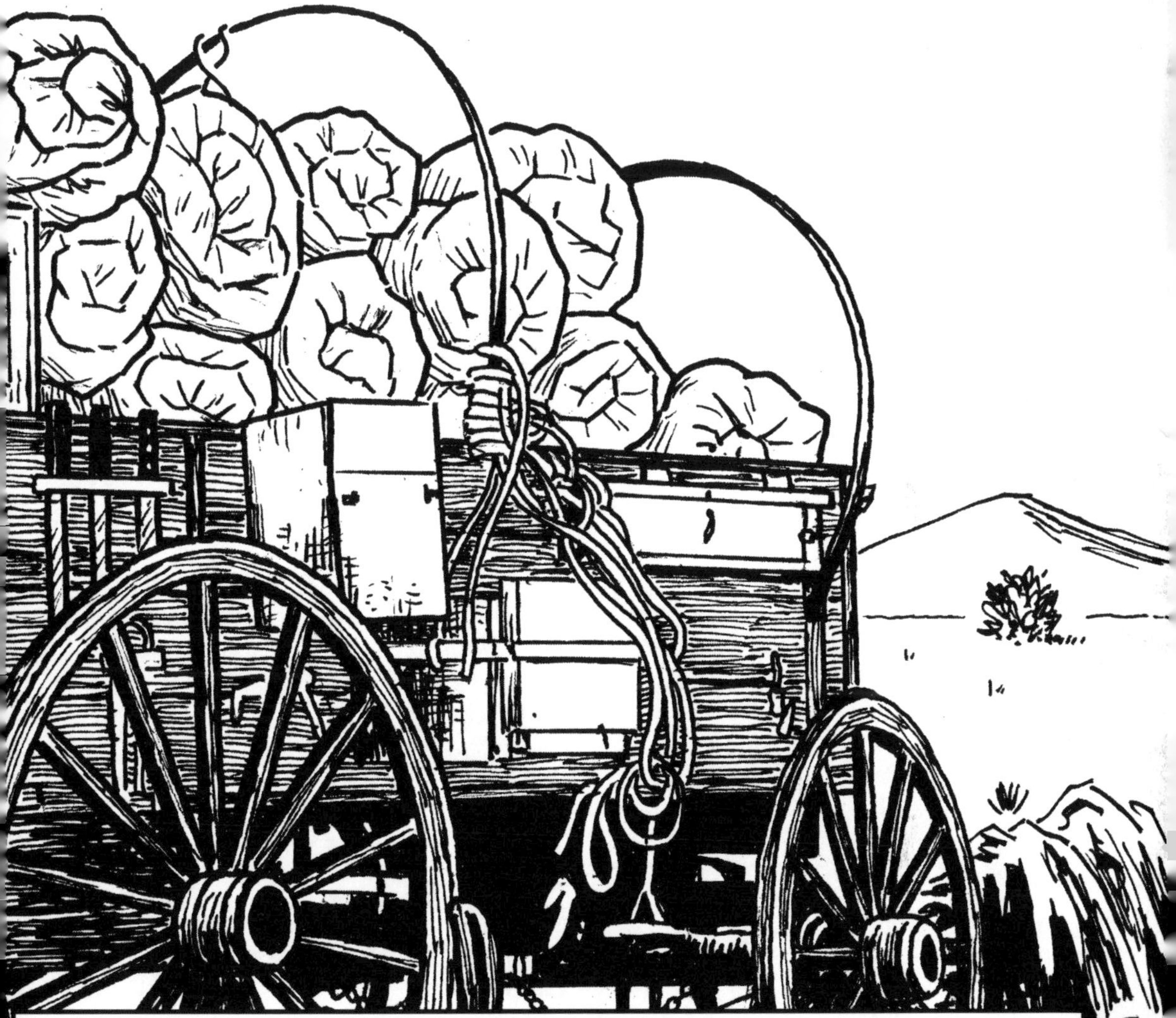

### TRAIL DRIVE STAPLE

BEEF, COFFEE, AND BISCUITS WERE STANDARD TRAIL DRIVE FARE. SOURDOUGH WAS A COWBOY FAVORITE. AT THE BEGINNING OF A DRIVE, THE COOK WOULD MIX UP A BATCH OF BATTER AND LET IT FERMENT IN A JAR. BISCUITS WERE MADE EACH MORNING BY ADDING SODA AND LARD TO THE FERMENTED BATTER. THE COOK CONTINUALLY ADDED MORE FLOUR, SALT, AND WATER TO HIS SOURDOUGH SO THAT THE FERMENTING PROCESS CONTINUED DURING THE ENTIRE DRIVE.

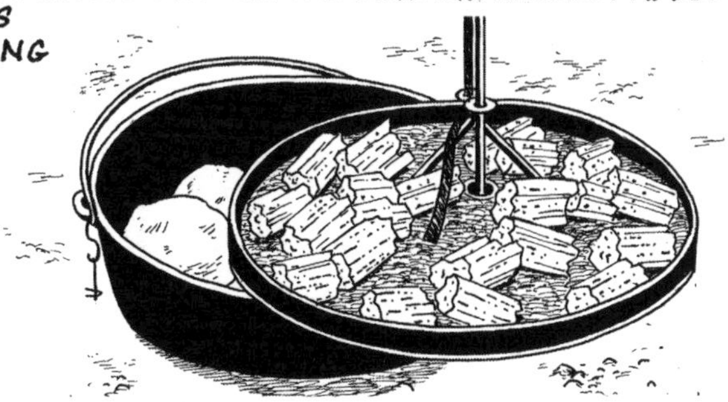

**SOURDOUGH BISCUITS**

2 cups flour
1/4 cup lard
1/2 teaspoon baking soda
1 teaspoon baking powder
1 teaspoon salt
1-1/2 cups fermented starter

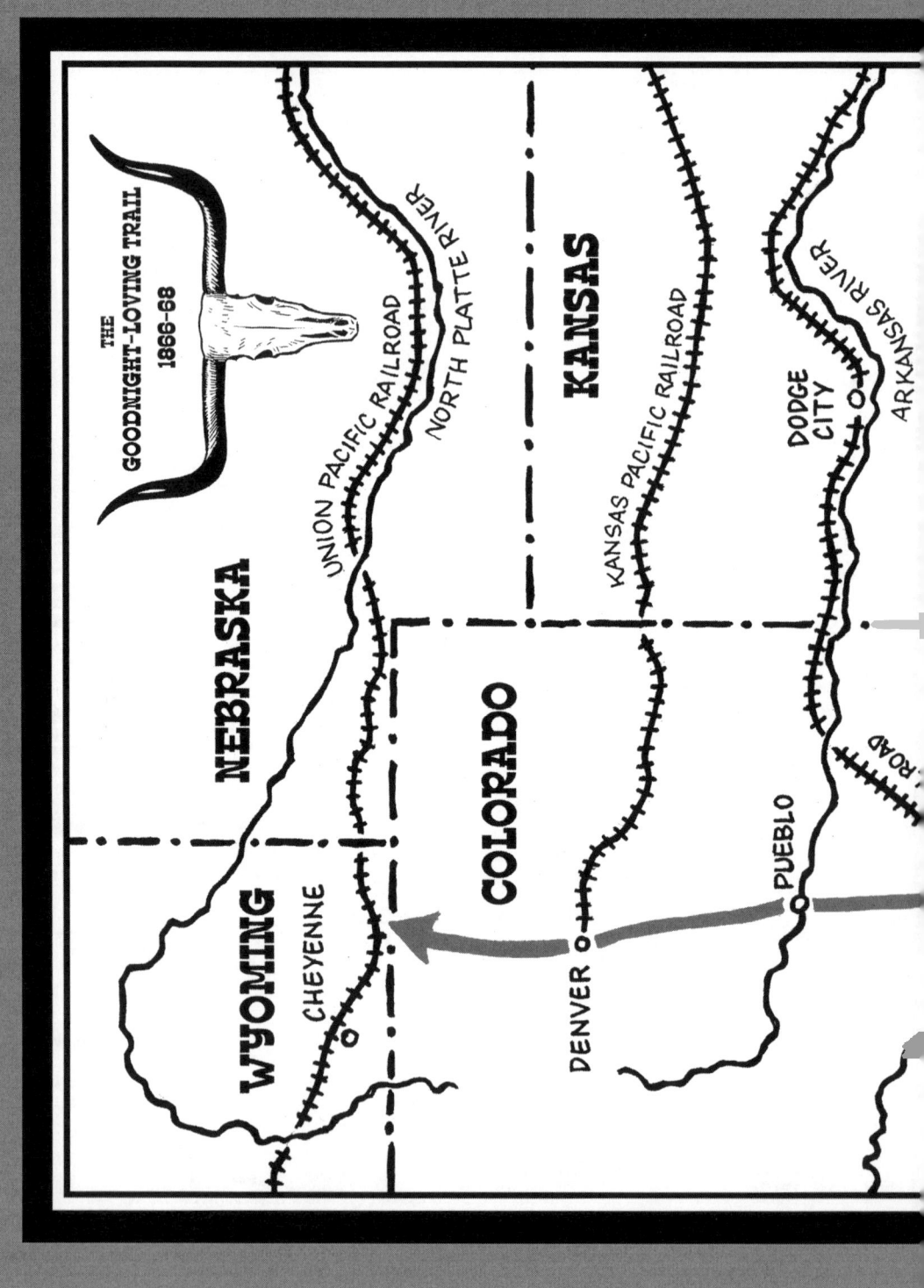

THE
GOODNIGHT-LOVING TRAIL
1866-68

NEBRASKA

WYOMING

CHEYENNE

COLORADO

DENVER

PUEBLO

KANSAS

DODGE
CITY

UNION PACIFIC RAILROAD

NORTH PLATTE RIVER

KANSAS PACIFIC RAILROAD

ARKANSAS RIVER

RAILROAD

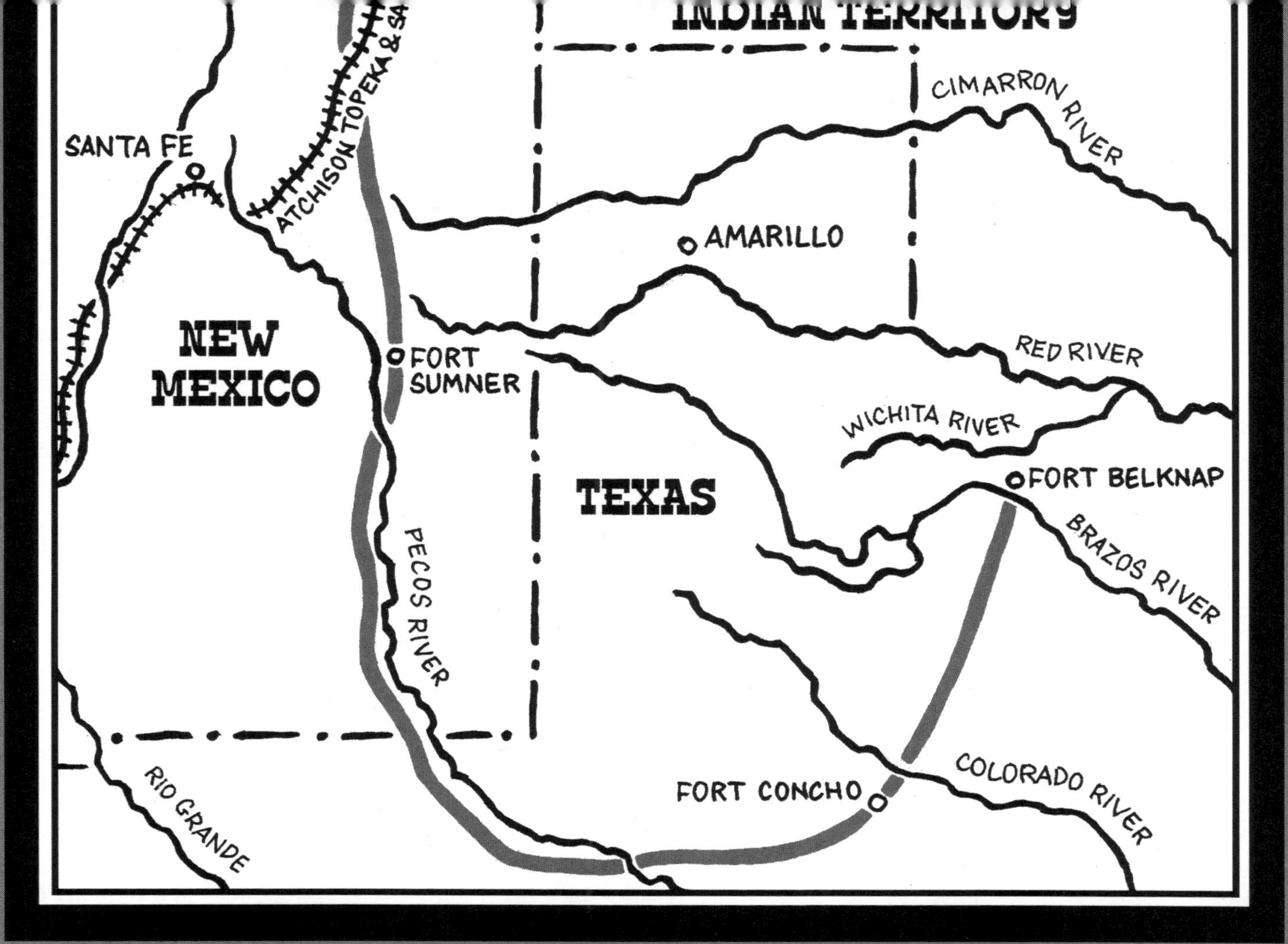
INDIAN TERRITORY
CIMARRON RIVER
SANTA FE
ATCHISON TOPEKA & SA
AMARILLO
NEW MEXICO
FORT SUMNER
RED RIVER
WICHITA RIVER
FORT BELKNAP
TEXAS
BRAZOS RIVER
PECOS RIVER
RIO GRANDE
FORT CONCHO
COLORADO RIVER

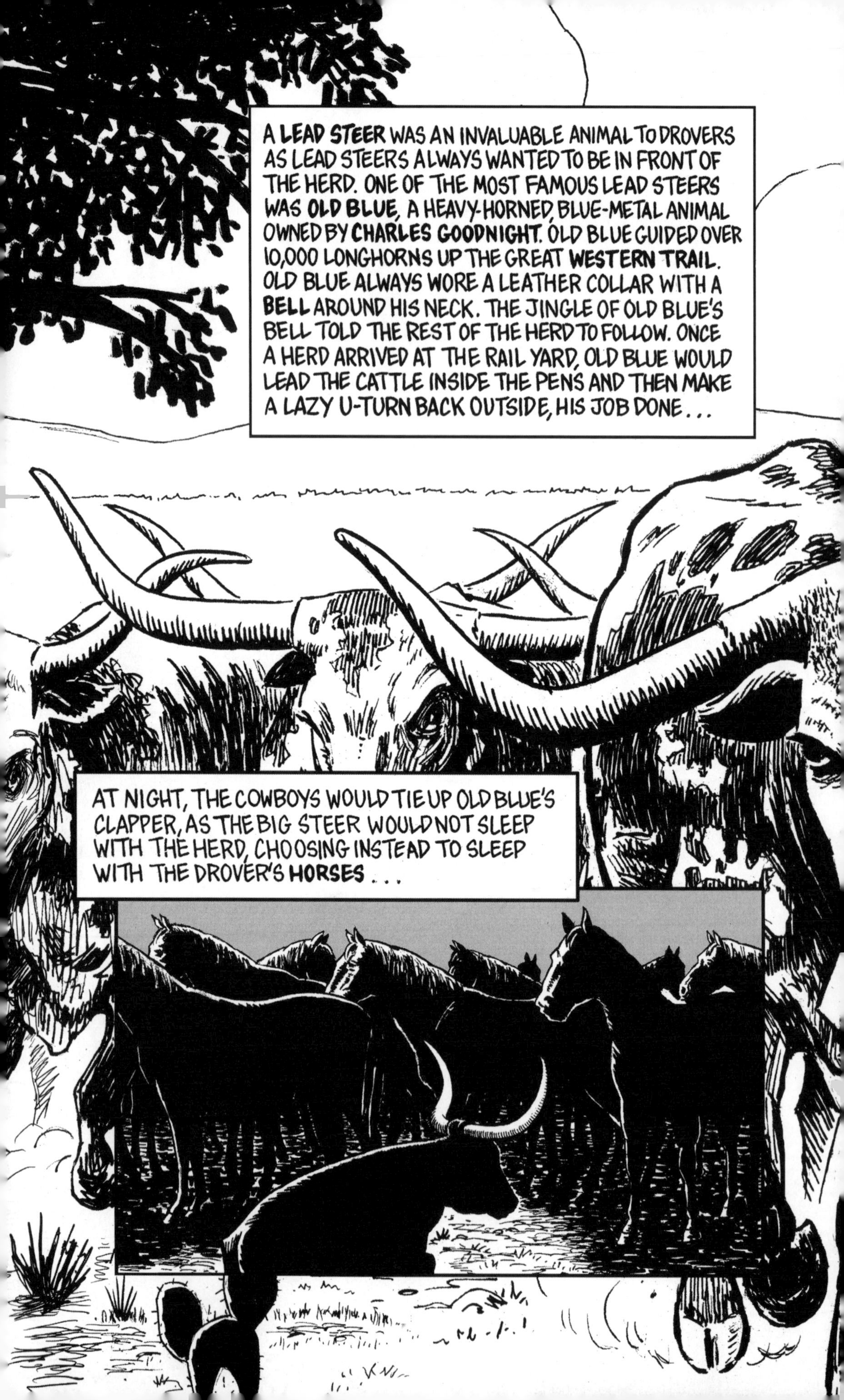
A LEAD STEER WAS AN INVALUABLE ANIMAL TO DROVERS AS LEAD STEERS ALWAYS WANTED TO BE IN FRONT OF THE HERD. ONE OF THE MOST FAMOUS LEAD STEERS WAS OLD BLUE, A HEAVY-HORNED, BLUE-METAL ANIMAL OWNED BY CHARLES GOODNIGHT. OLD BLUE GUIDED OVER 10,000 LONGHORNS UP THE GREAT WESTERN TRAIL. OLD BLUE ALWAYS WORE A LEATHER COLLAR WITH A BELL AROUND HIS NECK. THE JINGLE OF OLD BLUE'S BELL TOLD THE REST OF THE HERD TO FOLLOW. ONCE A HERD ARRIVED AT THE RAIL YARD, OLD BLUE WOULD LEAD THE CATTLE INSIDE THE PENS AND THEN MAKE A LAZY U-TURN BACK OUTSIDE, HIS JOB DONE...
AT NIGHT, THE COWBOYS WOULD TIE UP OLD BLUE'S CLAPPER, AS THE BIG STEER WOULD NOT SLEEP WITH THE HERD, CHOOSING INSTEAD TO SLEEP WITH THE DROVER'S HORSES...

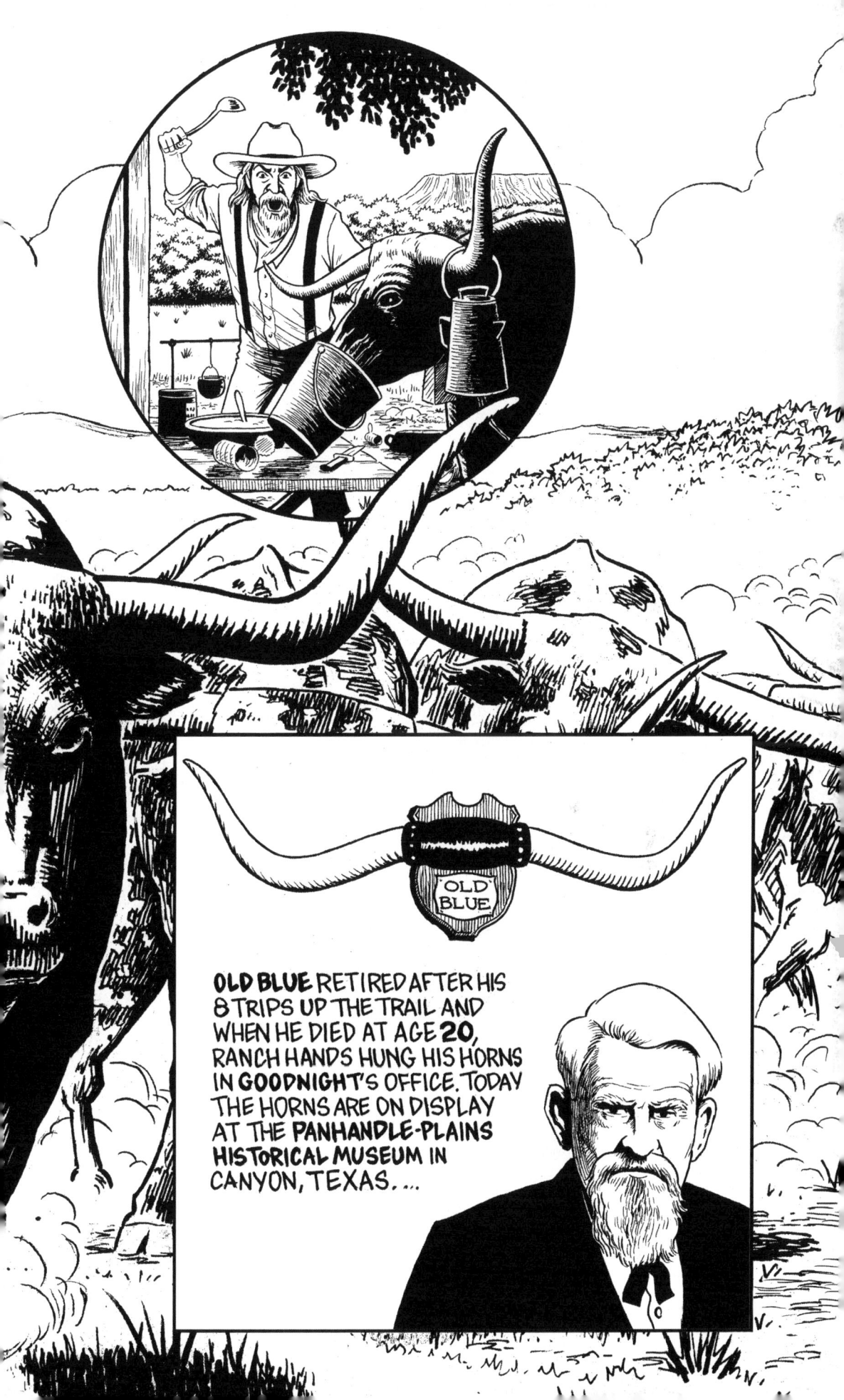

OLD BLUE RETIRED AFTER HIS 8 TRIPS UP THE TRAIL AND WHEN HE DIED AT AGE 20, RANCH HANDS HUNG HIS HORNS IN GOODNIGHT'S OFFICE. TODAY THE HORNS ARE ON DISPLAY AT THE PANHANDLE-PLAINS HISTORICAL MUSEUM IN CANYON, TEXAS. ...

OLD BLUE

IN 1867, **JOSEPH G. McCOY** LAUNCHES THE CONSTRUCTION OF A SHIPPING YARD, HOTEL, STOCK PENS, AND OFFICES IN **ABILENE, KANSAS.** McCOY ENVISIONS ABILENE AS A MEETING PLACE FOR NORTHERN BUYERS AND TEXAS DROVERS.

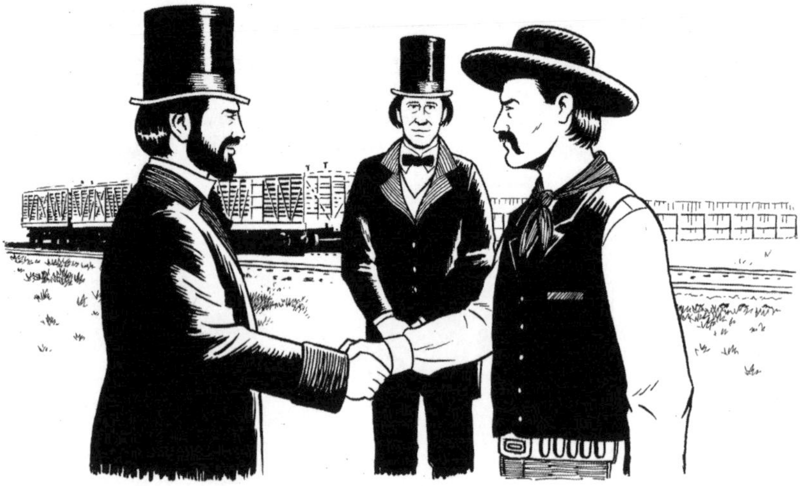

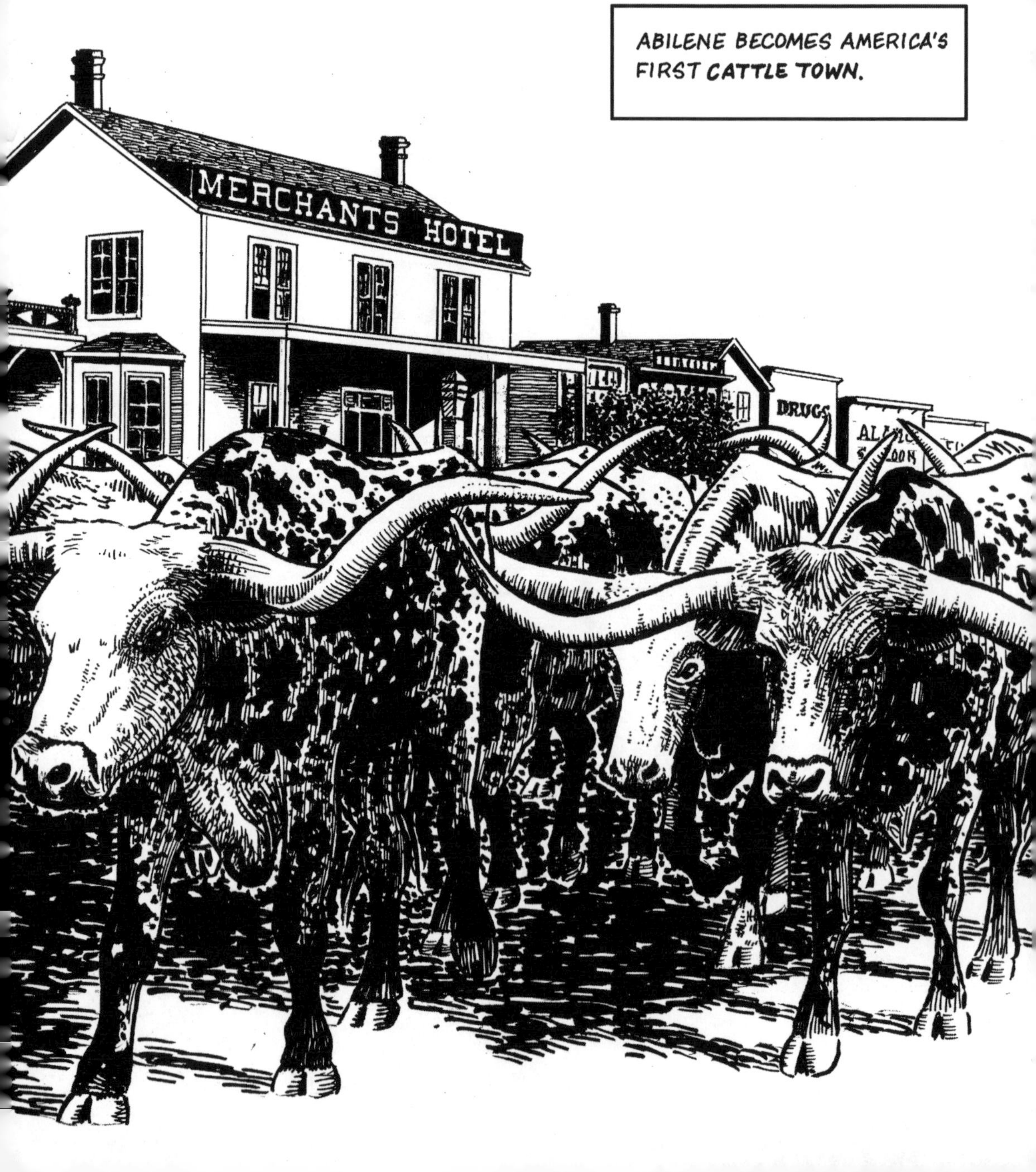
ABILENE BECOMES AMERICA'S FIRST **CATTLE TOWN.**
MERCHANTS HOTEL
DRUGS

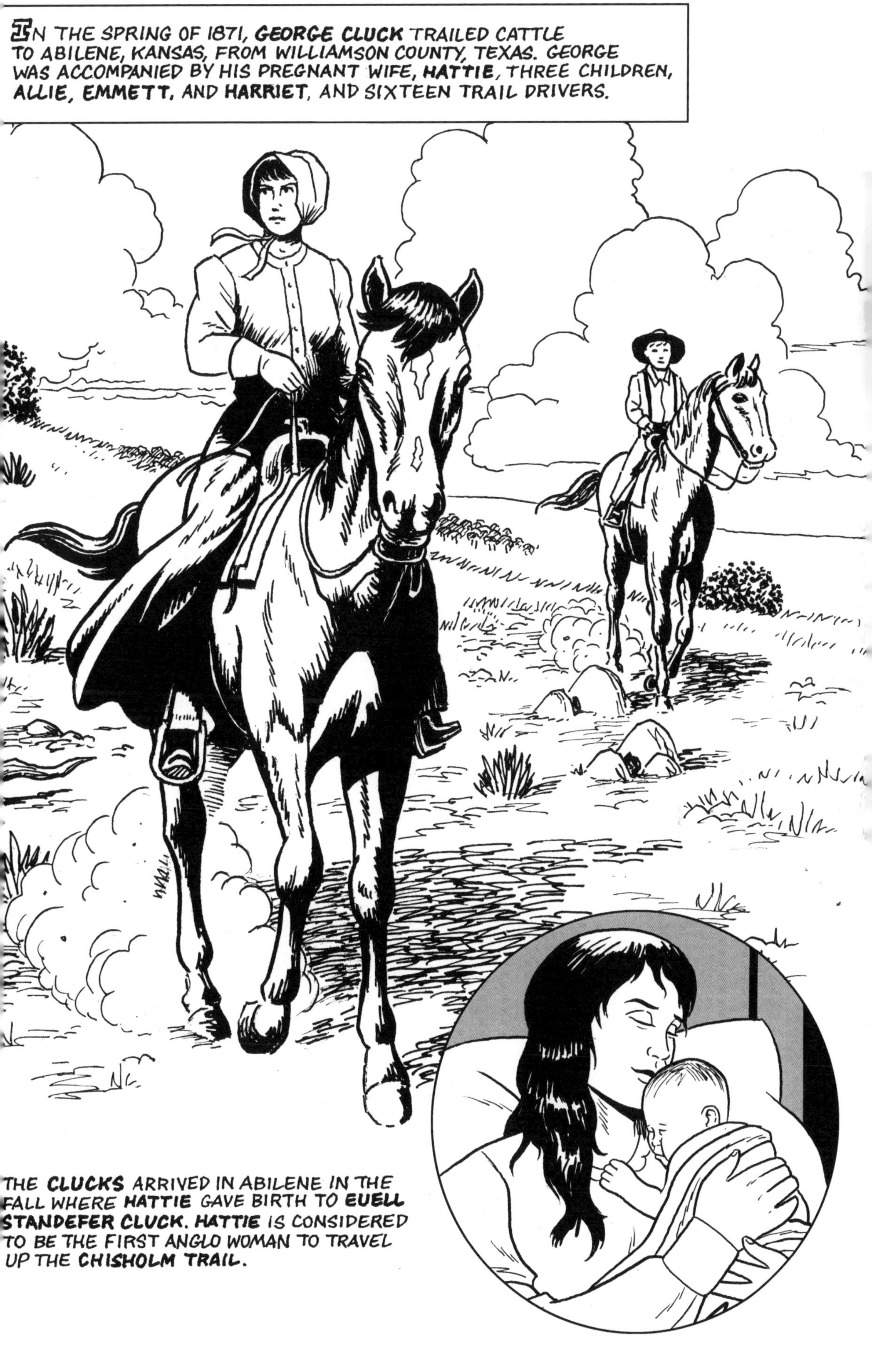
IN THE SPRING OF 1871, GEORGE CLUCK TRAILED CATTLE TO ABILENE, KANSAS, FROM WILLIAMSON COUNTY, TEXAS. GEORGE WAS ACCOMPANIED BY HIS PREGNANT WIFE, HATTIE, THREE CHILDREN, ALLIE, EMMETT, AND HARRIET, AND SIXTEEN TRAIL DRIVERS.
THE CLUCKS ARRIVED IN ABILENE IN THE FALL WHERE HATTIE GAVE BIRTH TO EUELL STANDEFER CLUCK. HATTIE IS CONSIDERED TO BE THE FIRST ANGLO WOMAN TO TRAVEL UP THE CHISHOLM TRAIL.

# HOW THE HERD MOVED

A TYPICAL TRAIL DRIVE LASTED TWO TO THREE MONTHS AND CONSISTED OF 10 TO 12 COWBOYS TO TRAIL A HERD OF 1,000 TO 3,000 TEXAS LONGHORNS 10-15 MILES A DAY.

### TRAIL DRIVE JOBS:

① **COOK** — DROVE AHEAD OF THE MAIN HERD. PREPARED 3 MEALS A DAY OUT OF THE BACK OF THE CHUCK WAGON. THE COOK'S DAY STARTED AT 3 A.M.

② **WRANGLER** — WAS IN CHARGE OF 60-70 SADDLE PONIES IN THE **REMUDA** HERD. (FROM THE SPANISH WORD "REMUDAR" MEANING TO EXCHANGE.) THE WRANGLER DROVE THE REMUDA HERD AHEAD OF THE MAIN HERD TO ENSURE THE REPLACEMENT MOUNTS ALWAYS FORAGED GOOD GRASS.

③ **TRAIL BOSS** — OVERSAW THE ENTIRE OPERATION, START TO FINISH. RESPONSIBLE FOR THE CATTLE AND THE COWBOYS.

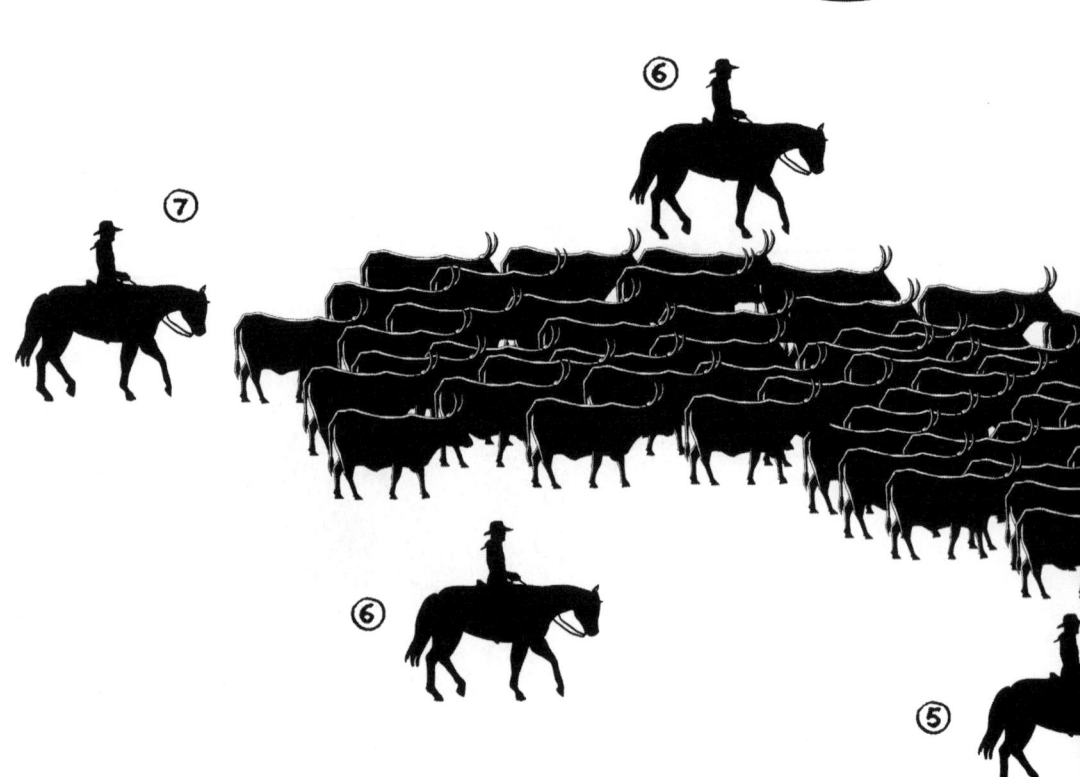

④ **POINT** — KEPT THE LEAD STEERS **POINTED** IN THE RIGHT DIRECTION.

⑤ **SWING** — RODE 1/3RD OF THE WAY BACK FROM THE POINT. KEPT THE BODY OF THE HERD MOVING WITH THE LEAD STEERS.

⑥ **FLANK** — RODE 2/3RD OF THE WAY BACK FROM THE POINT. KEPT THE MAIN BODY FROM SPREADING OUT TOO FAR.

⑦ **DRAG** — RODE AT THE BACK OF THE HERD. KEPT THE SLOWER CATTLE MOVING WITH THE HERD, HAD TO ENDURE ALL THE DUST KICKED UP BY 1,000 OR MORE STEERS.

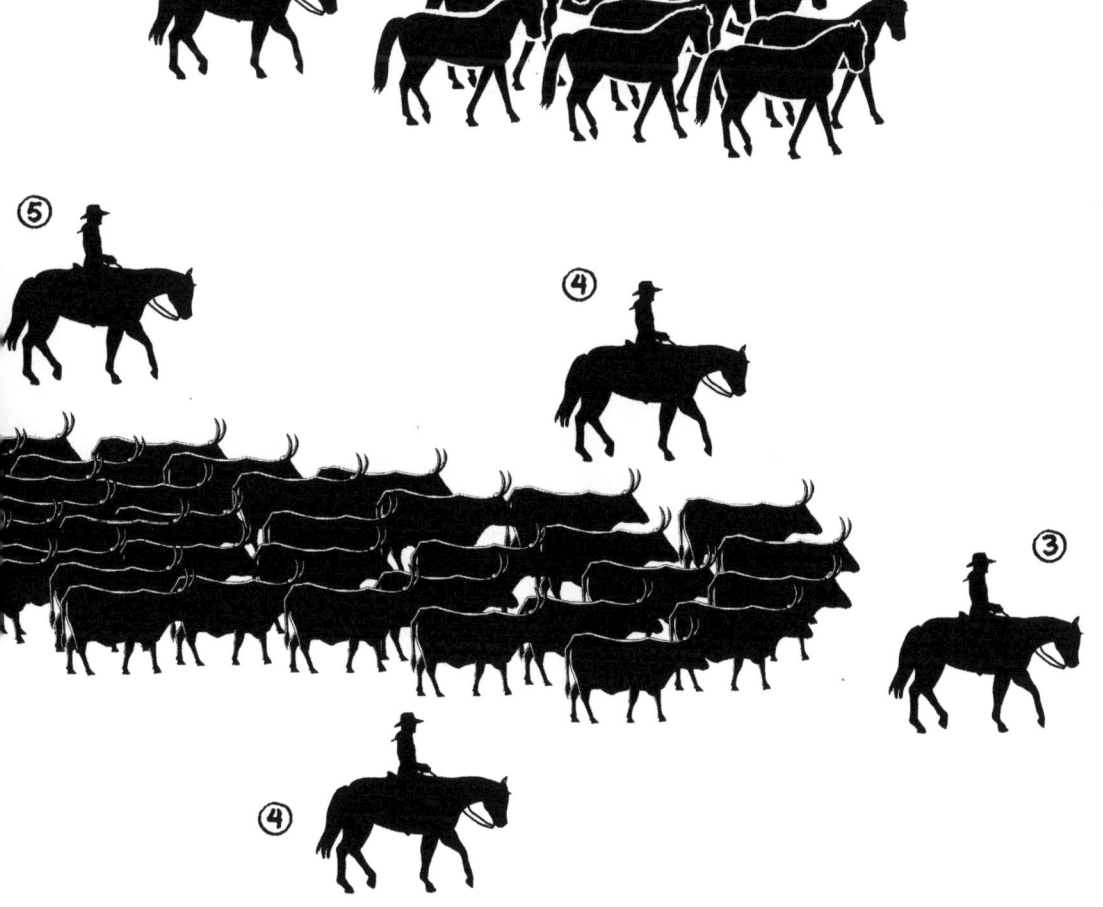

RUSTLERS, QUICKSAND, DROWNING, HAIL, LIGHTNING, AND THE SUDDEN **STAMPEDE** WERE ALL PART OF THE HAZARDS A COWBOY MIGHT FACE ON THE TRAIL. MANY A TEXAS COWBOY RELATED THAT THE CLOSER THE HERD DREW TO **KANSAS**, THE MORE LIKELIHOOD OF VIOLENT THUNDERSTORMS. DISTANT THUNDER AND A BLUE-GREEN SKY ON THE NORTHERN HORIZON MADE THE CATTLE RESTLESS AND ANXIOUS.

**E. C. ABBOTT** IN HIS BOOK, **WE POINTED THEM NORTH**, WROTE OF HIS ENCOUNTERS WITH LIGHTNING ON THE TRAIL, "I WOULD SEE IT FLASHING ON THE HORNS OF THE CATTLE AND THERE WOULD BE BALLS OF IT ON THE HORSE'S EARS AND EVEN MY MOUSTACHE, LITTLE BALLS ABOUT THE SIZE OF A PEA."

THE CRACK OF THUNDER AND THE SKY LIT UP BY LIGHTNING COULD TRANSFORM A MILLING HERD INTO A STAMPEDE IN SECONDS. A SPOOKED STEER MIGHT RUN FOR MILES BEFORE ONE OR TWO DETERMINED COWBOYS COULD BREAK THE HERD'S MOMENTUM.

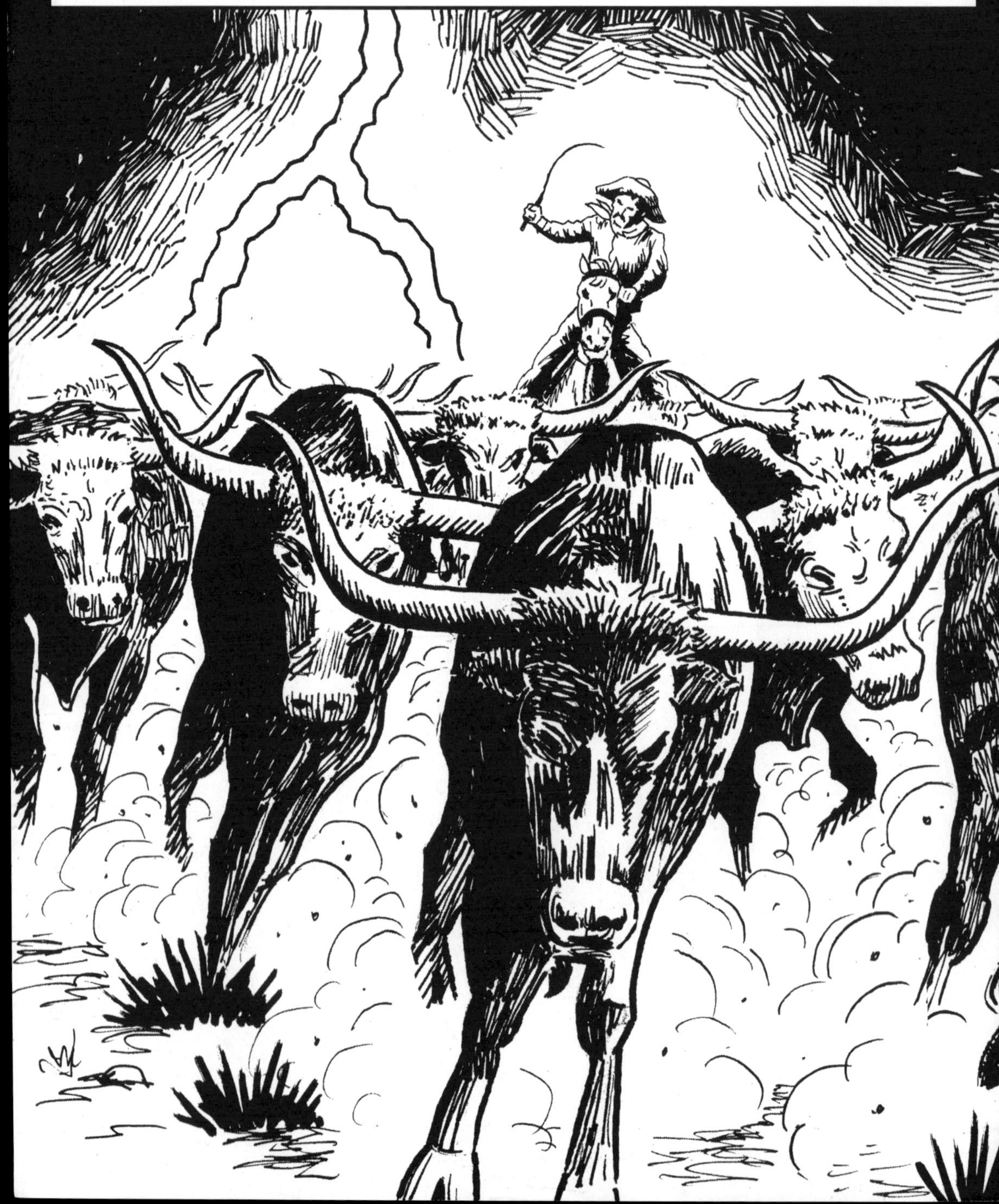

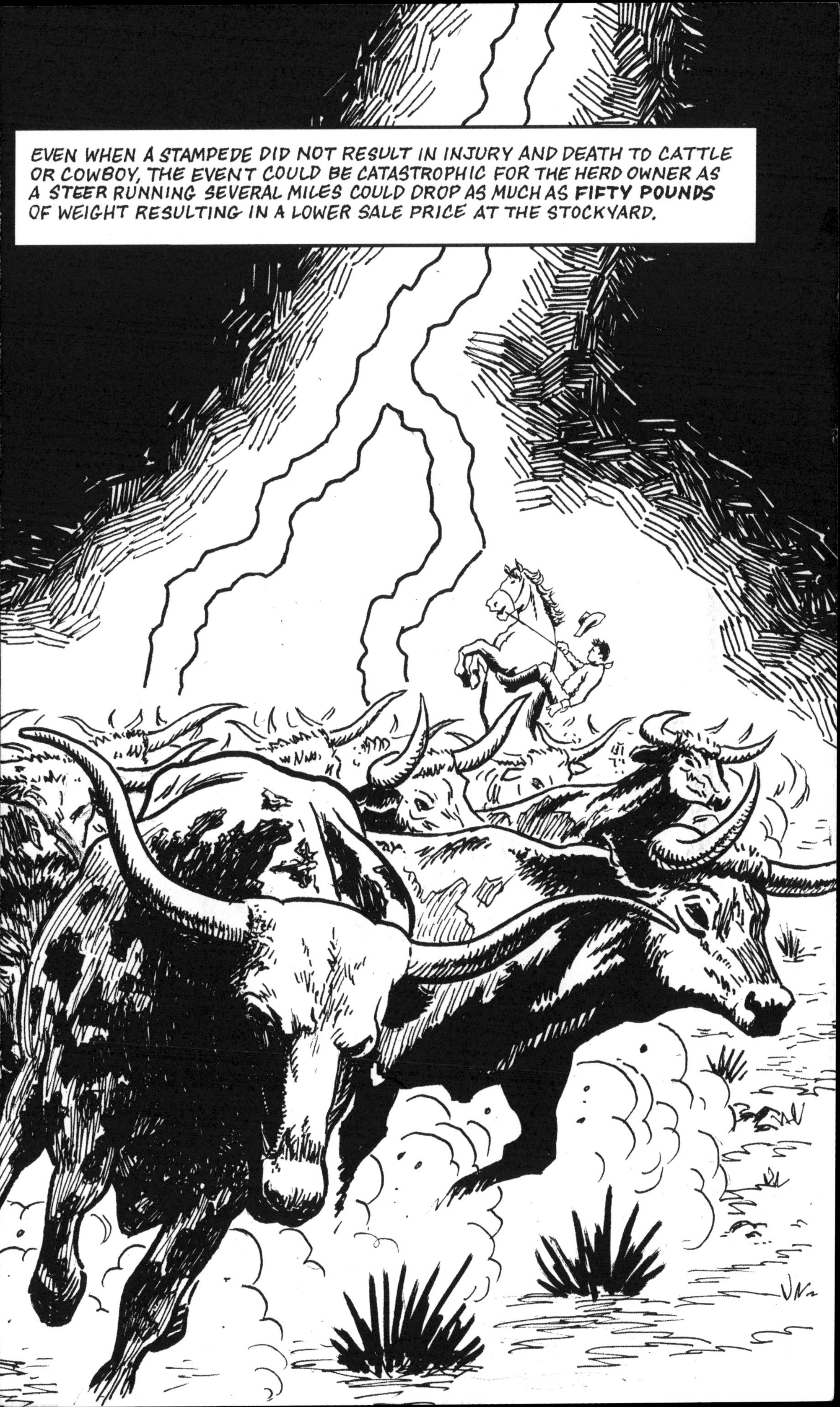
EVEN WHEN A STAMPEDE DID NOT RESULT IN INJURY AND DEATH TO CATTLE OR COWBOY, THE EVENT COULD BE CATASTROPHIC FOR THE HERD OWNER AS A STEER RUNNING SEVERAL MILES COULD DROP AS MUCH AS **FIFTY POUNDS** OF WEIGHT RESULTING IN A LOWER SALE PRICE AT THE STOCKYARD.

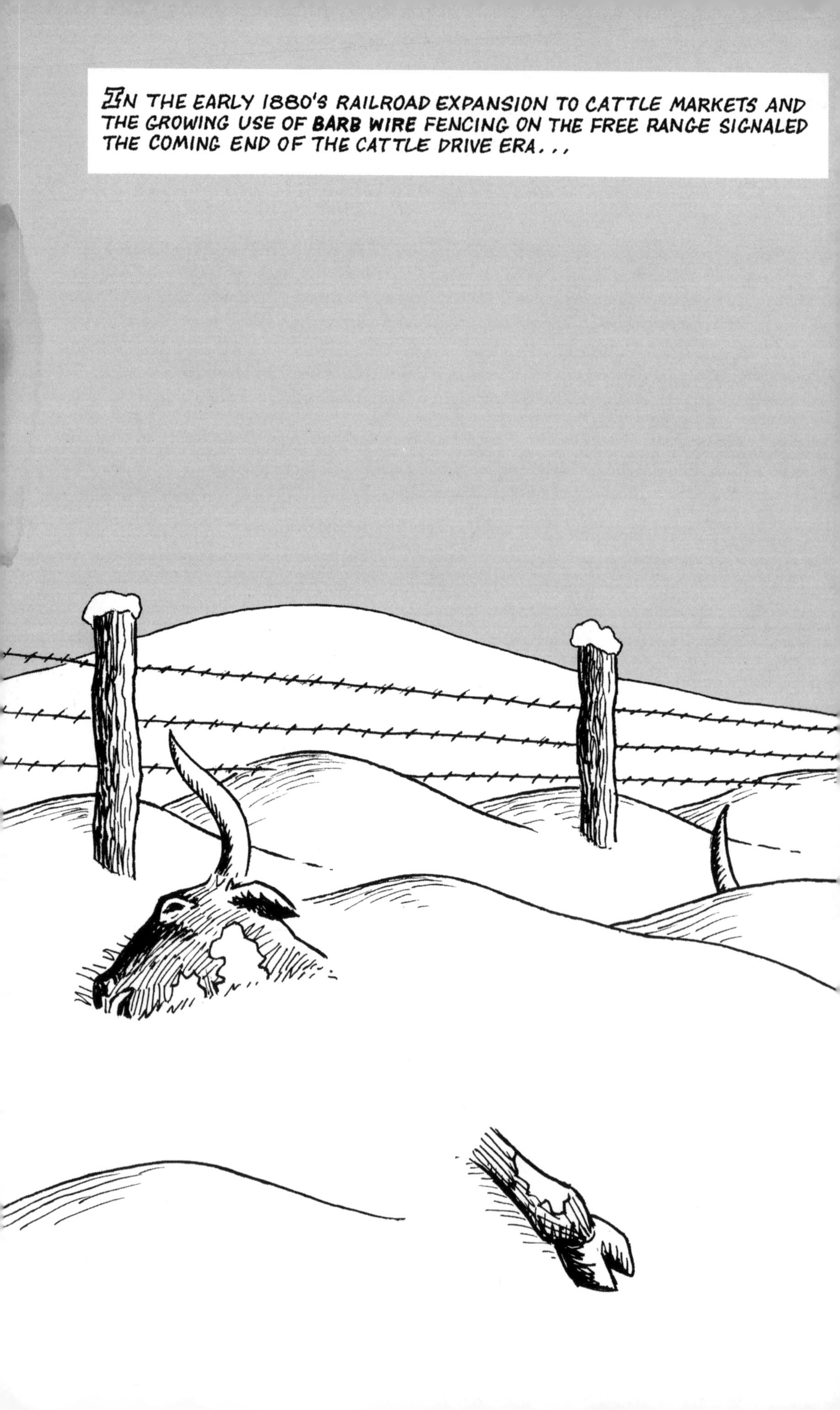
IN THE EARLY 1880'S RAILROAD EXPANSION TO CATTLE MARKETS AND THE GROWING USE OF BARB WIRE FENCING ON THE FREE RANGE SIGNALED THE COMING END OF THE CATTLE DRIVE ERA...

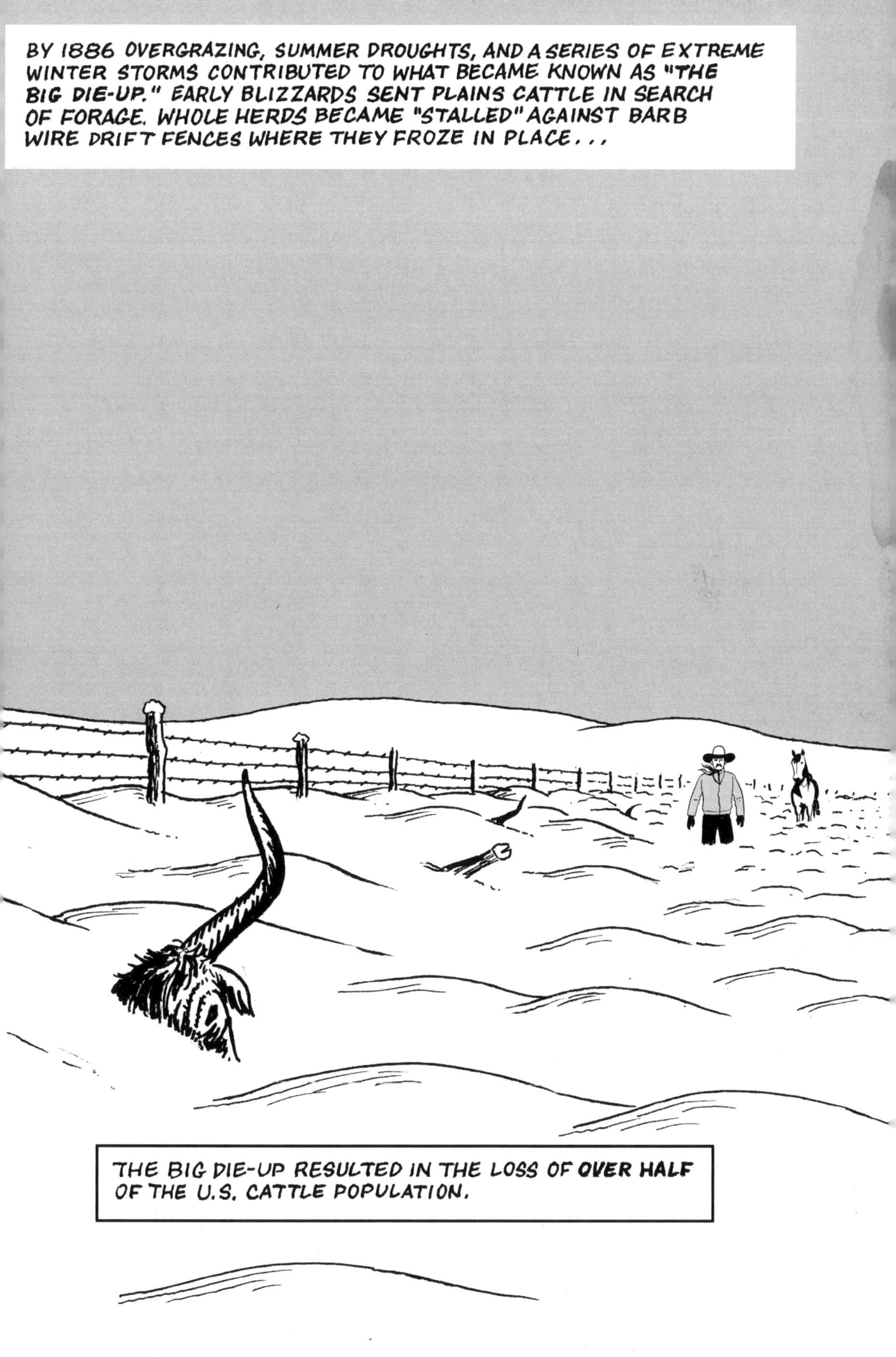
BY 1886 OVERGRAZING, SUMMER DROUGHTS, AND A SERIES OF EXTREME WINTER STORMS CONTRIBUTED TO WHAT BECAME KNOWN AS "THE BIG DIE-UP." EARLY BLIZZARDS SENT PLAINS CATTLE IN SEARCH OF FORAGE. WHOLE HERDS BECAME "STALLED" AGAINST BARB WIRE DRIFT FENCES WHERE THEY FROZE IN PLACE...
THE BIG DIE-UP RESULTED IN THE LOSS OF **OVER HALF** OF THE U.S. CATTLE POPULATION.

# SELECTED BIBLIOGRAPHY

**BOOKS:**

E.C. Abbott, Helena Huntington, *We Pointed Them North*. Norman: University of Oklahoma Press, 1954.

Lon Tinkle, Allen Maxwell, *The Cowboy Reader*. New York: Longmans, Green, and Co., 1959.

**INTERNET:**

H. Allen Anderson, "GOODNIGHT, CHARLES," *Handbook of Texas Online*, http://www.tshaonline.org/handbook/online/articles/fgo11, uploaded on June 15, 2010. Published by the Texas State Historical Association.

Jimmy M. Skaggs, "CATTLE TRAILING," *Handbook of Texas Online*, http://www.tshaonline.org/handbook/online/articles/ayc01, uploaded on June 12, 2010. Texas State Historical Association.

Kristina Gaylord, "Chisholm Trail," KansaPedia http://www.kshs.org/kansapedia/chisholm-trail/17155. June 2011. Kansas Historical Society.

H. Allen Anderson, "BIG DIE-UP," *Handbook of Texas Online*, http://www.tshaonline.org/handbook/online/articles/ydb02, uploaded on June 12, 2010. Texas State Historical Association.

Martha Deeringer, "Old Blue: Top Hand on the Trail," http://www.texascooppower.com/texas-stories/history/old-blue-top-hand-on-the-trail, January 2010. Texas Co-Op Power.